Original title:
The Spider Plant Sagas

Copyright © 2025 Creative Arts Management OÜ
All rights reserved.

Author: Julian Montgomery
ISBN HARDBACK: 978-1-80581-944-8
ISBN PAPERBACK: 978-1-80581-471-9
ISBN EBOOK: 978-1-80581-944-8

Draped in Green Elegance

In a pot so compact and tight,
A plant hangs down, oh what a sight!
With leaves like ribbons, a dance in the air,
Is it a plant or a stylist's chair?

Neighbors peer in, their eyes open wide,
Is that a pet or just plant pride?
A middle of tiny, green fireworks,
Who knew nature could throw such quirks?

Vines of Whimsy

Vines twirl around like they're on a spree,
Chasing the sunlight, happy as can be.
With a twist of leaves and a turn of stems,
Do they plot mischief like cheeky gems?

In corners they climb, all sneaky and sly,
Plotting their routes as they aim for the sky.
'Watch out for my leaves!' they humorously shout,
They'd twist your words, without any doubt!

Growing Together in Nature

In nature's arms, we sway and cheer,
A circle of greens, no need for fear.
We laugh at the bugs, a merry brigade,
Doesn't it feel like a grand parade?

Sharing the soil, our roots entwined,
Dreaming of sunshine, our hearts aligned.
With every breeze, we shimmy and shake,
Plant buddies forever, make no mistake!

Lush Chronicles

Gather 'round, folks, for stories galore,
Of leaves that gossip and roots that adore.
They chuckle at clouds and sunbeams that tease,
In a world full of plants, who needs expertise?

When rain taps a rhythm, the party begins,
Dancing in puddles, with giggles and spins.
The tales of the lush, oh they're quite absurd,
Just ask that fern who keeps tripping on words!

Lifeblood of the Leaf

In a pot, green leaves do dance,
Watering can gives them a chance.
They wag their toes in morning light,
Chasing shadows, what a sight!

With reckless glee, they stretch and sway,
Inviting mischief into play.
A gentle breeze gives them a spin,
Laughing leaves, let the fun begin!

Stories in the Roots

Deep down below, oh what a tale,
Roots tell stories, they rarely fail.
Tangled mess but full of cheer,
"Who needs a map? We're pioneers!"

They whisper jokes in the damp dark soil,
"Next stop, the watering can, let's toil!"
Adventures grand underneath the earth,
A hidden world of playful mirth.

Flourish Amidst the Chaos

Amidst the clutter, they take a stand,
Sprouting wildly, oh so grand.
"In chaos we grow," they cheer with glee,
"Who needs a gardener? Not even me!"

With pots that wobble and soil that spills,
They giggle while dodging all the drills.
Life's a mess, but oh so bright,
In every tumble, they find delight!

Woven Wonders

In balconies high, they string and twine,
Fashioned marvels, oh so fine.
Leaves twist together, a crochet dream,
"Look at us! We're the plant team!"

They lure the sun with a leafy grin,
"Join us, friend; let the fun begin!"
With each new sprout, laughter grows wide,
In woven wonders, we all abide!

Silent Webs of Green

In corners where shadows play,
A plant with style holds sway.
It stretches out, a leafy hand,
Swaying softly, oh so grand.

With tendrils long and wisdom vast,
It mocks the dust that clings from past.
Each leaf a tale, all true and bold,
Of houseplants brave, and stories old.

A spider nestled in its hair,
Wears a crown, without a care.
He weaves a laugh, a funny jest,
In the plant pot, he's a guest.

So if you spy this leafy show,
Just know there's more than meets the glow.
A giggle, twist, or playful dare,
In silent webs, they dance and share.

Legacy of the Leafy Dream

Green leaves piled like a dream,
In sunlight's warmth, they laugh and beam.
With every sip of rain or dew,
They grow more bold, as plants will do.

A rogue leaf swings on threads of sun,
Chasing shadows, just for fun.
They whisper secrets to the breeze,
And dance as if they were at ease.

In pots they plot their leafy schemes,
Creating worlds beyond our dreams.
With mischief sewn in every seam,
Life's simply better with a green team!

So let them bask in laughter bright,
These plants that bring such pure delight.
Their legacy? A life esteemed,
In every sprout, a giggle gleamed.

Tendrils of Time

Tendrils curling, what a sight,
Reaching high to grasp some light.
Time stands still for leafy glee,
As they wiggle, wild and free.

In pots they weave their silly tales,
Of broken pots and friendly snails.
The sunbeams dance, a round of fun,
Each leaf a smile, each stem a pun.

Planted stories start to brew,
With every whisper, a new debut.
They plot and play, they scheme and tease,
In their leafy world, they do as they please.

So if you find your heart in twine,
Remember, plants are quite divine.
With tendrils that giggle and sway,
They brighten up the dullest day.

Whispers in the Soil

In the soil, a secret hum,
A party rages, oh so fun!
Tiny roots tap dance along,
In the dark, where they belong.

Each earthy whisper, light and bright,
Sings of growth through day and night.
A leafy crown, a little tease,
Leaves sway softly, with gentle ease.

With every pot, a tale unfolds,
Of playful leaves and roots so bold.
A comedy of errors there,
As plants decide just where to share.

So listen close, and you shall find,
The laughter buried, intertwined.
For in that soil, where mischief coils,
Are whispers wrapped in playful spoils.

Green Symphony in Fragments

In pots where green dreams hide,
The leaves dance side to side.
With water, they greedily drink,
Turning sunshine into shrinks.

A leaf once tried to play guitar,
But twirled too much, oh what a star!
With spiders jumping, they swayed,
In a concert, how they played!

One day a rogue leaf took a leap,
Making the whole plant weep.
"Oh dear, stop that silly prance!"
But it just wanted to romance.

So here we sit, within our greens,
In whispered jokes, and funny scenes.
Nature's jesters, bright and spry,
We laugh and laugh as time goes by.

Luminous Leaves and Hidden Stories

Underneath the sun's warm glow,
Lies a world we barely know.
Leaves whisper tales of days gone by,
Filling the air, oh my, oh my!

A curious sprout decided to climb,
Meet the cat — oh, that was prime!
With flicks and fluffs, they shared a snack,
A battle of wits, no holding back!

Silly stalks spreading joy like cream,
Making their way into every dream.
They giggle and huddle, never apart,
An orchestra playing the sun-kissed heart.

In pots they live, a jolly crew,
With stories crafted just for you.
So sit and listen, stay awhile,
To laughter within a leafy smile!

Webs of Green Dreams

In a corner, plants collide,
Creating webs where secrets hide.
With every twist and every turn,
A lesson learned, so absurd to discern.

Leaves telling tales of silly fights,
Between the shadows and the lights.
"I swear I saw a bug pass by!"
One exclaimed with a shameless sigh.

Oh, the drama of pot and soil,
Pugs and cats make the mischief boil.
For every leaf with dreams to spin,
There's a spider crafting ways to win!

In networks fine, they weave with flair,
Drawing giggles from the air.
With tangled fun, the stories beam,
Life's a hoot, unfurl the dream!

In the Tongue of Leaves

Whispers rustle through the greens,
Every leaf with hidden dreams.
"What's the gossip?" one leaf said,
"Did you hear about the cat who fled?"

In leafy tones, the tale unfolds,
Of daring deeds, and secrets bold.
An ant wearing boots, a runaway rat,
Oh, the silliness of it all, imagine that!

Roots tickle under soil's embrace,
Planting giggles in their place.
With every wiggle and sway of the stem,
Life's a comedy, a greenish gem!

So join the laughter, let it spread,
In the world where greens are wed.
With every joke, every playful tease,
The tongue of leaves brings joys with ease!

Threads of Lush Lullabies

In a pot on the sill, a dancer sways,
With leaves like ribbons, it plays all day.
Swinging to sunlight, what a setup,
You'd think it's practicing for a dance-up!

Tiny sprouts sprout in delightful rows,
Jiving and thriving, just look at that pose!
They wiggle and giggle, a green circus crew,
Their leafy parade is sure to amuse you!

When watering's needed, they throw a splash,
A leafy high-five, nature's own bash.
With roots that are tangled like jokes on a page,
These plants keep on laughing, age after age!

In this leaf-laden drama, they acrobat,
A leafy crescendo, imagine that!
Filled with laughter, they dream and they grow,
Nature's own jokers, putting on a show!

Echoes in the Quiet Corner

In the corner sits a green little sprite,
Whispering secrets in the soft moonlight.
With a wink and a stretch, it tickles the cat,
Who jumps with a yowl, what was that?

The whispers of leaves rustle with glee,
Telling the stories of you and of me.
With little green threads, a tapestry spun,
They giggle together, oh what fun!

Things fly by in this quiet retreat,
A cozy lil' space where laughter's a treat.
Watch as the dust motes perform a ballet,
While the plant chuckles, "Come dance, come play!"

So here in the corner, laughter had grown,
With friends in the shadows, never alone.
As long as they're rooted, their giggles will stay,
Nature's own joke, in a green, leafy way!

Nature's Whispering Heart

A heart of green giggles, a breath of fresh air,
With comrades in pots, they've formed quite a pair.
The sun sits and swoons, casting shadows so bright,
While the leaves share their stories, through day and through night.

Bouncing around with a jolly old cheer,
They chat with the breeze, "Hey, come over here!"
Each leaf a comedian, they tell all the jokes,
Even the roots join in, in their deep, leafy folks.

With a swirl and a laugh, they dance in their space,
Creating a ruckus, a wild leafy chase.
While the world rushes by in its busy old way,
The plants gather for laughs, come what may!

So join in the fun with this nature-based art,
In every small leaf beats a whispering heart.
In laughter we thrive, in nature we trust,
With joy all around, we gather in rust!

Portraits of Perseverance

In pots piled high, with eyes on the sky,
Grows a band of leaves, not shy, oh my!
With each twist and curl, a story unfolds,
Of courage and giggles, of dreams yet untold.

When tangled, they chuckle, a gang of sheer will,
Stretching for sunlight, and climbing up still.
Their roots dig deep, through the muck and the mire,
Who knew that plant life could dance and inspire?

Through rains and through droughts, they never give in,
Each leafy resilience, a wink and a grin.
In tenacity's portrait, they paint the delight,
Of how leafed ambitions can soar to new heights!

So raise up a glass to the green and the brave,
To laughter and courage, the joy that they pave.
In the world of the plants, where humor abounds,
Perseverance has never been this fun to be found!

The Urban Eden

In a corner pot, a sprout appears,
Whispering secrets, calming our fears.
With a twist and a turn, it reaches for light,
Claiming the space in a playful fight.

Its leaves wave high, doing little dances,
Inviting us all to take silly chances.
Neighbors peek in, curious yet shy,
Wondering if it can teach them to fly.

Chasing dust bunnies, plotting for fun,
In the world's wild mess, it's second to none.
A jester in green, with humor so spry,
In this urban garden, watch worries fly by.

Follow the Green Path

There's a vine that climbs, with a mind of its own,
Mapping the room like it's setting the tone.
In timid delight, it coaxes a grin,
As it stretches and twists, intending to win.

With pots all around, it's a whimsical race,
Plant friends high five in this leafy embrace.
A party unfolds on the shelf, oh my!
Don't trip on the roots, just let laughter fly.

In the sunlight's glow, they chime and agree,
To aim for the heights, as high as the tree.
Each leaf shares a joke, they chuckle just right,
In this green adventure, everything's light.

Time in a Terrarium

Within glass walls, a jungle resides,
Time meanders, while the plant slyly hides.
It binds up the past and dances with mirth,
A botanical realm where the giggles have worth.

With soil as the stage, the roots take a bow,
A tiny performance, come see it right now!
The moss does a jig, the ferns sway and whirl,
In this quirky habitat, watch nature unfurl.

Days spin around, but they rarely get bored,
With butterflies laughing, and earthworms adored.
In this confined world, hilarity rules,
Crafting moments of joy, as nature's own fools.

Trellis of Time

On a trellis of dreams, the plants climb and peek,
Whispering tales of the heights that they seek.
With humor and charm, they tickle the air,
In a leafy bazaar, with gossip to share.

Each tendril a jest, curving up to the sun,
Telling the stories of battles just won.
They weave through the hours, with laughter and cheer,
Growing from whispers and giggles sincere.

As time takes a turn, the green crew conspires,
To play pranks on shadows and challenge their fires.
In this timeless space, let the fun thrive,
With vibrant green nonsense, we're truly alive!

Celestial Canopy

In a pot on the sill, it dreams so grand,
Leaves reaching out like a magician's hand.
Chasing sunlight like a playful sprite,
It dances and wiggles, a curious sight.

With roots like a traveler, exploring below,
Holding secrets of where all its friends grow.
Poking fun at the ferns, it can't help but tease,
Swaying in breezes with the utmost ease.

Its children cascade, like a green waterfall,
Making a mess that's a joy for us all.
Gossiping to the dust bunnies at night,
Those plants have stories that tickle delight.

Oh, to be a spider – that's quite the jest,
Creating a jungle, putting patience to test.
An architect of chaos, but we love it so,
In the land of our windows, it puts on a show.

Twisted Tales of Growth

Once there was a sprout with a penchant for fun,
Playing hide and seek with the old grandmother's sun.
Each leaf went on adventures, plotting at dawn,
As they whispered of mischief before they were gone.

Sister roots dived deep, searching for snacks,
While the leaves up top threw extravagant hacks.
Judging by laughter, it seems they're quite bold,
With wild tales of wisdom, forever retold.

One day they conspired to stretch on the rack,
Curling and twisting, they just wouldn't look back.
A game of confusion for the hapless old chair,
While the dog gave a sigh, quite aware of their flair.

When daylight retreats, and night starts to sing,
These leafy comedians prepare for their fling.
For in their small world, they've woven a web,
Of giggles and tales, all tucked in a ebb.

Leafy Legends

In the kingdom of pots where laughter does bloom,
Legends are sprouting, shaking off gloom.
A tap dance of roots, a waltz with the light,
Each day is a saga, a cheerfully bright.

Sir Leafy the First claims the sunniest spot,
With his knights made of vines, they didn't know what.
They giggled and jostled, teasing the air,
Telling tall tales of their botanical flair.

Princess Fern rolled her eyes at their cheer,
While Mr. Cactus just sat, sipping his beer.
"What's all this fuss? Can't a plant catch a break?
With all this ruckus, I'd soon start to quake!"

But the leafy legends laugh louder each night,
As they form a grand circle, basking in light.
With roots intertwined, it's a party of glee,
In the garden of dreams, there's always a spree.

Resilience Woven with Green

In the tapestry of life, green threads intertwine,
Each leaf a reminder, like a sip of caprine wine.
With wisdom of ages, they stretch and they twist,
Playing peek-a-boo with mist, like a playful tryst.

Through storms and sunbeams, they've weathered them all,
Standing so proud, never ready to fall.
With laughter as nutrients, they bloom with delight,
Crafting their stories, one leaf at a night.

Unruly and funny, with tendrils galore,
They wiggle through mornings, always ready for more.
A resilient brigade, full of whimsical dreams,
In this green house of giggles, nothing's as it seems.

For among all the greenery, life laughs and rejoices,
They share their grand plans with bumbled voices.
Each day a new chapter, each night a green scheme,
In the wonder of growth, they shine like a dream.

Nestled in Nature's Hands

In a pot so round and wide,
A leafy creature does reside.
With a twist and a jaunty jig,
It stretches out, oh so big!

Tiny spiders all around,
This plant has secrets unbound.
It whispers tales of sunlight,
While dancing with pure delight!

When watering, it's quite a sight,
Splashing leaves like a frolic flight.
A little drink, a hearty cheer,
The plant giggles, have no fear!

In corners where shadows dwell,
It throws a party, ringing bells.
Inviting all that pass its way,
To join its leafy cabaret!

Roots of Resilience

Beneath the soil, roots take hold,
Winding stories yet untold.
They dance beneath the earth's cool skin,
In a world where silences spin.

Every twist, a tale they weave,
With leaves above that never grieve.
They beckon bugs, they challenge fate,
In the garden, they celebrate!

The world may shake, the pots may sway,
But resilience finds a way.
With a giggle, they stake their claim,
Spreading joy in nature's game!

Through seasons bold, they stick around,
With roots that dance beneath the ground.
A raucous crew of green delight,
In every nook, they spread their light!

Green Threads Unraveled

With threads of green, they like to tease,
A playful dance on the morning breeze.
Each tendril sways, a silly show,
As if they're strutting to and fro!

They twist and twirl through pots and cracks,
In little hats, they hold their snacks.
A guffaw rises from the leaves,
As sunlight weaves through midday eves.

Spilling over with leafy cheer,
They welcome every passerby here.
A comedy of nature's grace,
With playful charm, they claim their space!

Unraveled threads, a splendid spree,
Where laughter sings wild and free.
For in their midst, joy finds a way,
To brighten up the dullest day!

Tangled in Light

In beams that dance and skip around,
This verdant crew has tightly wound.
They bask and bask, a sunlit retreat,
With leafy giggles, oh so sweet!

Some say they're tangled, I say refined,
In chaos, friendship you will find.
Each twist a tale, each knot a laugh,
Sunlight's glow, a leafy gaffe!

When shadows loom, they play the game,
In every storm, they stake their claim.
With roots that tickle, leaves that sway,
They charm the clouds to dance and play!

So here's to greens, our leafy friends,
With every laugh, their joy extends.
In nature's light, they find their glow,
A tapestry of fun to show!

Potted Dreams Unfurled

In a pot so bright and round,
Little leaves dance without a sound.
They sway to tunes of sunlit rays,
In their verdant world, they play all day.

With a twist and turn, they stretch up high,
Whispering tales to the curious sky.
They hoot and they holler, a leafy delight,
Chasing the shadows, embracing the light.

Tiny tendrils reach for the feast,
A gathering of dust bunnies, to say the least.
They giggle and wiggle, nothing's too grim,
In their potted dreams, they never get dim.

So here's to the green, the quirky, the sweet,
In their little kingdom, life's a treat.
With a flourish and flair, they bloom and twirl,
In a pot of laughter, the dreams unfurl.

Nature's Heartbeat

In a world where leaves go boom,
A frolic of ferns makes up the room.
With roots that tickle and leaves that cheer,
Nature's heartbeat is loud and clear.

When the wind howls like a playful pup,
Plants start dancing, getting pumped up.
They strut their stuff in a green parade,
Making it fun, never afraid.

As raindrops fall like tiny clowns,
The garden wears its best of gowns.
Each petal giggles, each stem does sway,
In nature's rhythm, they frolic and play.

So let it rain, let the sun shine bright,
Nature's heartbeat brings joy and delight.
With every pulse, every rustle, every leap,
It sings a song that's ours to keep.

Balance in the Botany

In a pot, they stand in a green ballet,
Each leaf a dancer, in grand array.
With roots beneath, grounding their wits,
They twirl and twist, doing funny skits.

The sun pokes in, all cheeky and bold,
While shadows linger, brief stories told.
In the light, they giggle, in the shade, they hum,
In balance they thrive, a botanical drum.

As they reach for the sky with leafy charms,
They giggle and sway in delightful arms.
In this circus of green, no act is the same,
Each moment's a joke, each plant a name.

So here's to the balance, a dance of the greens,
In pots full of laughter, no room for routines.
With a flip and a flop, they keep it alive,
In the wacky world of plants, we thrive!

Traces of Tenderness

In a leafy abode where whispers blow,
Each leaf a secret, tucked in a row.
They giggle softly, in sunlight's embrace,
Traces of tenderness, a warm bright space.

A little insect dances, a curious guest,
Plants chuckle and query, "Who's this, a pest?"
Yet with a nod and a playful grin,
They share the turf, let the fun begin!

When evenings drape in a silken thread,
The plants tell stories of the day that's fled.
With each gentle rustle, a giggle, a sigh,
Traces of tenderness linger nearby.

So let's toast to the plants, so quirky and free,
In their playful realm, oh, what joy to see!
With every flicker of a leaf, they say,
In this dance of life, we laugh and sway!

Melodies of the Indoor Jungle

In the corner, green twists and sways,
On curious nights, it sings and plays.
A dance of leaves in fluorescent glow,
Who knew plants had talent, though?

When visitors come, they mock it sly,
"That pot's just sitting!" they say and sigh.
But whisper sweet nothings, oh what a sight,
It croons back softly, 'I'm groovin' tonight!'

The cat jumps up, a surprising foe,
Pawing the leaves, stealing the show.
Yet amidst the chaos, a laugh is found,
As the leafy musician spins round and round.

Roots underground, a secret so deep,
The rhythm pulses, a plant's nightly leap.
In the jungle of home, we all play our part,
Grooving together, a beat from the heart.

Cultivating Calm

In cozy pots, they quietly churn,
Waves of oxygen our lungs yearn.
Grow lights shine bright like disco's gleam,
Plants prance about, living the dream.

Potted pals with a thirst for chat,
Whispering secrets to the watering cat.
With every sprout, a chuckle is found,
As they giggle softly, rooted to ground.

When schedule's tight and days bring the stress,
They nod their leaves, saying, 'Don't you fret!'
So, I take a seat and share a cup,
Breathe in their vibe, and just lift up.

In this green sanctuary, happiness pours,
Nature's cheerleaders, they open doors.
With each little leaf, they gently embrace,
The chaos of life, a gentle place.

The Language of Photosynthesis

Photosynthesis, what a quirky tale,
Green factories buzzing, never pale.
They sip the sun, in joyful flesh,
Buzzing and whirring, in greenish mesh.

Carbon dioxide, their favorite dish,
Filling their bellies, oh what a wish!
Turning light into laughter, such crafty glee,
Chlorophyll's magic, setting them free.

In this leafy world, a witty exchange,
As they chat in shades, a little derange.
'Breathe easy, friend! Let's make some air!'
With their chlorophyll smiles, they show they care.

Each little sprout, a wise little sage,
Spinning sunlight into art, page by page.
So when you see them, give a hearty cheer,
For these leafy scholars, we hold so dear.

Serenity in Each Sprout

A tiny sprout on the window ledge,
Yells, 'Hey! I'm here! Time to pledge!'
With roots like noodles, it stretches wide,
Inviting all gloom to take a ride.

Whispers of green in a still, calm room,
The air thickens sweet, banishing gloom.
Fingers dance through leaves, a ticklish spree,
Each sprout a giggle, just wait and see.

Across the shelf, a cactus stands proud,
Wearing its spines like a spiky shroud.
Yet share a laugh, and oh what a show,
As plants gossip softly, their secrets flow.

In serenity found, plant pals unite,
Bringing peace and joy, day and night.
So here's to the greens, both wild and stout,
In every small sprout, laughter's about.

The Botanist's Confession

I bought a green friend, a leafy delight,
In love with the pot, oh what a sight!
But watering it daily? A real grand quest,
It drowned in my care, I'd never have guessed.

Oh, laughter erupted when it turned brown,
Was it a plant or a wilted old gown?
I whispered my secrets, it stood up so proud,
Yet each failed attempt brought giggles out loud.

Those leaves took a tumble, a dramatic flair,
I tried to revive it with maximum care.
But alas, it just wobbled, a travesty true,
A plant with more drama than I ever knew.

So here's to my buddy, who's now just a ghost,
In memory's garden, it's loved the most.
I'll cherish its charm in a whimsical way,
A botanist's blunders, a funny bouquet!

Tales of Tenacity

In a corner it sat, a survivor so bold,
With leaves like a treasure, a sight to behold.
It twisted and turned, defying the odds,
I cheered on my green friend like it was the gods!

Each morning I'd come, and it'd sprout with glee,
My little green warrior, oh can't you see?
While friends had their cacti and blooms all around,
Mine was a legend, the best in the ground!

Yet one fateful day, it took quite a leap,
Off the shelf, oh dear! Into soils so deep.
I rushed to revive it, but fate would decide,
A tumble so funny, I laughed as it cried.

Now tales of its courage are shared near and far,
A plant with a spirit more wild than bizarre.
Such is the journey, full of giggles and fun,
A chronicle leafy, never to shun!

Beneath the Shade of Leaves

Beneath a canopy of greens, I found,
A world of giggles, where laughter's abound.
With sunlight beaming, the mischief began,
As I played little games with my leafy friend, Stan.

I'd whisper sweet secrets, they'd rustle with glee,
Telling tales of the wind and the honeybee.
But one day, dear Stan started shaking his head,
I'd forgotten the water, "Now look what you've bred!"

"Oh no, my dear friend, are you feeling unwell?
Should we throw you a party, or ring a loud bell?"
He leaned to the side, as if in despair,
I burst into laughter; he was quite the flair!

So here in the shade, we'd giggle and weave,
Life's small little moments that we both believe.
In the laughter of leaves and the bright sunny rays,
We spun our own stories and danced through the days!

Verdant Stories Intertwined

In a jungle of pots, with plants intertwining,
A comedy blossomed, quite whimsical, defining.
Every leaf had a tale, every vine had a laugh,
Together they plotted, a green autographed path.

With chlorophyll dreams, they reached for the sky,
A botanist's canvas, oh how they'd fly!
But every adventure brought a twist of the fun,
Like swinging on tendrils, a green whirlwind run.

"Oh! Not too much sun!" cried the timid old fern,
While the cactus stood proud, with a cheeky little turn.
They danced in the breeze, a funny parade,
Each moment a memory, a leafy charade.

So here in my garden, the tales intertwine,
Of plants full of laughter, both silly and divine.
In this verdant domain, with giggles we chime,
Creating our stories, one leaf at a time!

Climbers of the Homebound Horizon

In a pot by the window, they stretch and sway,
Green little ninjas plotting their play.
With leaves outstretched for a daring climb,
They conquer the sill, one twist at a time.

They whisper of journeys on sunny rays,
Dreaming of gardens in bright ballet.
But gravity laughs at their leafy ambition,
As they wiggle their roots with sweet inhibition.

They chatter of heights where the clouds go,
Yet end up tangled in search of a show.
With wiggly tendrils like silly fingers,
They weave their tales where adventure lingers.

So toast to the climbers, so bold and spry,
As they strut on the sill, reaching for the sky.
In pots full of laughter, they take their chance,
Making every hour an indoor dance.

Ephemeral Blossoms Unfurled

A curious sprout with playful flair,
Decides it's the time to flaunt and share.
Little buds pop like a burst of joy,
Each bloom a giggle, no hint of coy.

They talk of the sun and long, lazy days,
Blushing with laughter in sunbeam rays.
With a wink and a nod, they sway to the beat,
Of indoor symphonies, oh what a treat!

A parade of petals, in colors so bright,
They prance and they twirl, a strange indoor sight.
But wait, what's that? The neighbor's cat stalks!
These brave little flowers double their talks!

They whisper and giggle under the leaves,
Evading the paws of furry thieves.
In luminescent laughter, they bloom and they twirl,
Creating a ruckus in their leafy whirl.

A Symphony of Indoor Breezes

In the corners of rooms, a breeze likes to play,
It dances with fronds in a whimsical way.
With rustles and chuckles, it sways to and fro,
As leaves gossip secrets, no one ought to know.

They gather in circles, a leafy debate,
On who gets the sunshine or who'll turn fate.
With tips of their fingers, they point and they tease,
Claiming the best spot with utmost of ease.

A gust with a giggle may knock them about,
Yet laughter remains as they twist all about.
An orchestra playing on the window ledge,
Rooting for humor with nature's own pledge.

So let's raise a cheer for the curl and the whorl,
As they twine in the music of wind's merry swirl.
An indoor ballet of green and of whim,
With breezes performing, and spirits so dim.

The Art of Airy Growth

In the art of growing, they leave no chance,
With each little sprout, they hop and prance.
Adventurers green with a daring grace,
Spreading their leaves in a leafy race.

"Stretch here!" cries one, as it jabs at the air,
"Just a bit more," another shouts, "if you dare!"
In a garden of giggles, they bloom with glee,
Racing for sunshine, a sight to see.

Tangled together, they share their big dreams,
In a world of shadows, they dance with beams.
With the humor of roots just a tangle or two,
And stories of growth that giggle and coo.

So gather 'round closely, and laugh with the green,
For the art of their journey is truly a scene.
With winds at their backs and space to explore,
They write out their tales, never craving for more.

Green Threads of Connection

In a pot of chaos, they wiggle and sway,
Finding the sunlight in a most cheeky way.
Green fingers extending, like fingers at play,
Grabbing their neighbors, oh what a display!

A spider's ambition, so bold and so spry,
Leaping from ledges as if it could fly.
Each tendril a story, a twist, and a sly,
Whispered giggles echo beneath the blue sky.

Chronicles of the Unseen

In the shadows they plot, with secrets to share,
A green brigade giggling without a care.
Dancing on shelves in a wild, wavy flair,
Living the life, like they're mostly up there.

The dust bunnies murmur with envy and fright,
As these leafy acrobats leap left and right.
Each twist is a tale, a whimsical flight,
Bringing laughter to all with their green-painted sprite.

Gentle Giants of the Shelf

Shelves are their kingdom, a leafy parade,
Gentle giants lounging, no need to invade.
With every soft sway, they charm and they aid,
Household banter, a comic charade.

Potmates in mischief, they conspire and scheme,
Plotting great pranks like a green-fingered dream.
Chasing the sun with a whimsical beam,
In this world of green, nothing's as it seems.

Tapestry of Home and Heart

Weaving their magic with each leafy thread,
Crafting a tapestry where laughter is spread.
Hanging out freely, no worry about dread,
Home's cozy corners adorned in green spread.

Moments of joy in the simplest things,
With whispers of humor that nature still brings.
In the heart of the home, where happiness clings,
They remind us of life's very humorous flings.

Secrets of the Pot

In a pot so round, so bright,
Little leaves dance in the light.
They whisper secrets, oh so sly,
And giggle as the days pass by.

Roots beneath in a tangled spree,
Plotting mischief, just wait and see.
With a sprinkle and a dash, they scheme,
Living life like a wild dream.

Friends with pests and spiders near,
They throw a party, bring the cheer.
Climbing high, they reach for the sky,
Just don't ask them how or why.

In their leafy world, they reign,
With endless joy and little pain.
So here's a toast, let's raise a cup,
To those green friends who lift us up!

Coils of Color

In the sun, they twist and twirl,
Green ribbons swirl and curl.
Each one flaunts its vibrant hue,
A leafy dance, a bold debut.

With laughter in their leafy veins,
Shaking off the morning rains.
Who knew plants could be so spry,
With a wink and a playful sigh?

Their pots are portals, seeds of fun,
Boys and girls, all on the run.
A jungle party, come all aboard,
With vines and leaves, a pranked accord.

As colors clash, the laughter grows,
In the garden, anything goes!
So join the coils, sway and play,
In a world where plants lead the way!

Flourishing in the Vital Flow

In every drop of morning dew,
A giggle hidden in the blue.
Roots and leaves conspire to grow,
In a dance that steals the show.

Sunbeams tickle, breeze does twirl,
Making every pot a whirl.
A botanical ball, on display,
Where green dreams spring out to play.

Water's laughter fills the air,
As tendrils stretch without a care.
Each sprout a star, blooming bright,
In a comedy of pure delight.

So let them flourish, let them shine,
In leafy laughter, they entwine.
A green parade of quirky glee,
In every pot, such joy to see!

Spirited Saplings

Tiny tales in pots abound,
Spirited saplings dance around.
With every leaf, a story grows,
Of wiggles, giggles, and garden shows.

In a party of flora, they convene,
Each playful sprout a lively scene.
Roots with dreams, and leaves that sing,
In a world where happy grows on spring.

They trade the secrets of the soil,
While sharing jokes, their hearts uncoil.
With a wink, a nudge, they plot their prank,
Making mischief that's never blank.

Together they will sway and cheer,
In the sunlight, their path is clear.
These spirited pals in green attire,
Bring joy to every pot, never tire!

The Guardian's Embrace

In the corner, you stand proud,
Always eager, a leafy crowd.
Sentinel of my little space,
With green fingers, you embrace!

Chasing dust with gentle grace,
Silently judging every face.
A guardian with leaves so bright,
Who knew house plants could take flight?

You whisper tales of sun and shade,
In every breath, a serenade.
Though jokes of browning leaves take flight,
You wear your quirks, and that's just right!

So here you sway, my favorite friend,
With humor, you always transcend.
In this jungle of pots and cheer,
Your hilarious antics bring good cheer!

Patrons of the Potted

In your realm of soil and stone,
You reign with glee, never alone.
A motley crew of greens and hues,
Laughing at our plant care blues.

Each leaf a cap, each stem a throne,
Mocking us while they've clearly grown.
We water with love, they thirst for jest,
In this kingdom, they stand the best.

Ferns giggle as we trip and fall,
While cacti poke with a knowing call.
"You think you're in charge?" they tease with mirth,
"Oh, human friend, we rule this earth!"

So let us raise a pot in cheer,
To leafy friends we hold so dear.
In this potted world, where laughter thrives,
Together, we all blossom and jive!

Journey of the Tiny Tendril

Once a seed, so small and meek,
You stretched your limbs, a daring peak.
Through soil dark, your quest began,
In search of sun, a leafy plan.

Twisting here, and curling there,
A comical dance, no need for care.
With every stretch, you tickle space,
A fractal beauty with a funny face.

Chasing light, a greedy reach,
Waving high as if to teach.
"Hello, world! See all my flair,
I'm here to charm, and none compare!"

So wander forth, brave little sprite,
In every leaf, there's pure delight.
Your funny path, a winding tale,
Of little joys in every scale!

Daring to Stretch

With an elbow up, you reach for fame,
A daring dance, a leafy game.
In sunny corners, you stretch with glee,
Funny how neighbors envy thee!

Each inch you grow, you pull a prank,
Displacing dust, the world went blank.
Branches flailing, it's quite the sight,
Caught mid-bounce, it's pure delight!

Swing low, swing high, what a display!
Bending rules in your leafy way.
"Look at me!" you shout with pride,
In this grand show, let's enjoy the ride!

So stretch and sway, in your own style,
With every leaf, you bring a smile.
In this jungle of whimsy and fun,
You're the jester, second to none!

Spirals of Growth

In a pot just for me, I'm feeling quite spry,
With curling green arms reaching up to the sky.
I dance like a noodle, all wiggly and free,
Photosynthesizing while sipping my tea.

Oh, look at my siblings, they mimic my flair,
We twirl in the sunlight, without any care.
A leaf here, a shoot there, we're building a crowd,
A circus of greens, oh, isn't it loud?

Backflips and cartwheels, we boast on the shelf,
In the living room light, we're a raucous old self.
The world thinks we're plants, but we know the truth,
We're just little ninjas, full of leafy goof!

So cheers to our spirals, to heights we will scale,
With roots in our pots, we'll never go stale.
Sprouting out laughter, we'll grow and we'll thrive,
In this jolly green circus, we're truly alive!

Escape from the Concrete

In this jungle of bricks, I wriggle and sway,
With leaves like confetti, I'll find my own way.
A dash past the builder, a leap past the grate,
I'm more than a plant; I'm a daring escape!

Through cracks in the sidewalk, my tendrils will creep,
Just like a magician, not a sound, not a peep.
With utmost precision, I'll reach for the sun,
The concrete might grumble, but look what I've done!

A garden of laughter, I start to create,
With every small sprout, I'll celebrate fate.
No more in a pot or confined to this plight,
I'm the king of the sidewalk, it's my leafy night!

So here's to the freedom, the sun on my face,
I'm a plant on a mission, I'll win this wild race.
Together we'll flourish, when all is said and done,
With roots like adventurers, we'll bask in the sun!

Embrace of the Epiphyte

I cling to the branches, a snug little brat,
With my fuzzy green cloak, I'm a happy acrobat.
Perched on the bark, I'm a curious sight,
A cozy green bug, never losing the fight.

The rain drops like candy, my own little shower,
In the hug of the tree, I feel all the power.
Swinging with laughter, I laugh with the breeze,
Oh, life up above, it's such a tease!

Each leaf is a story, each twist is a game,
I'm the quirkiest guest, never one to be tame.
The sun and the shadows, they play hide and seek,
As I dangle and sway, I have all that I seek!

So here's to the branches, to life in the air,
With every soft rustle, I know I'm in there.
An epiphyte jester, in my leafy parade,
I'll dance on the limbs, every role I've made!

Silent Symphony of Leaves

In the hush of the night, we sway to a tune,
With shimmering leaves, we'll be dancing till noon.
Whispers of green skies surround every hue,
As snippets of laughter weave melodies true.

A symphony played with the rustle of fronds,
Conducted by breezes, we're never beyond.
No need for a drummer, our petioles sway,
With the moonlight as spotlight, oh, we love to play!

So join in the fun, grab a leaf or two,
We'll spin and we'll twirl, it's a wild leafy brew.
Invisible maestros, we all take our part,
In this silent ballet, we dance from the heart!

So listen closely now, as we sing through the dark,
A whimsical chorus, we'll leave our spark.
For leaves that are singing are never alone,
In the dark of the night, we'll forever be known!

Lush Dreams in Ceramic Pots

In a pot so bright and round,
Green dreams of joy abound.
Tiny tendrils reach for glee,
Whispering laughs, 'Come dance with me!'

Water splashes, soil's delight,
In this garden, all feels right.
A curious bug drops by to peep,
In this lush jungle, secrets keep.

With every leaf, a tale unfurls,
Of plant parties and tiny swirls.
Ceramic friends in a wild dance,
Sprouting smiles at every chance.

Mossy hats on every head,
In this place, we fear no dread.
Potting soil has magic might,
Turning gray days into bright!

Legacy Woven in Leaves

Leaves whisper tales of yore,
Of a time when plants did soar.
With each curl and twist we see,
    A legacy of hilarity!

Grandma's secret in her stew,
Was a plant that always grew.
With laughter, it would bounce and sway,
    Crafting jokes in a leafy way.

Spirographs in vibrant hue,
Nature's art with a herbs' view.
Each strand is woven just with glee,
    In this leafy dynasty.

We're the jokers of the pots,
Crafting smiles, connecting dots.
A legacy not lost in dreams,
But woven deep in planty schemes!

Harmonies of the Urban Oasis

In the city, a jungle grows,
Where laughter blooms and life flows.
Pots align in quirky rows,
Creating music as breezes blow.

Cacti strum their spiny strings,
While daisies dance and joy sings.
Urban greens in a playful tease,
Tickling hearts just like a breeze.

Chimes of leaves in the sun's glow,
Tick-tock of nature's show.
From rooftop highs to sidewalk lows,
This harmony of fun just flows.

Neighbors gather, sharing smiles,
In this oasis, laughter piles.
Urban greens in all their splendor,
Creating moments to remember!

Breath of the Verdant Guardian

In the corner sits a sage,
A leafy one—no wooden cage!
Guardian of giggles and cheer,
Winking at troubles, bringing near.

With each breath, it spreads delight,
Filling rooms with soft, green light.
Whispers of jokes in the leaf's curl,
A funny twist with every twirl.

A shadowy friend, always near,
In its presence, we shed a tear—
Of laughter, joy, and playful scenes,
Breezy moments in vibrant greens.

So here's to the guardian, bold and bright,
Bringing smiles with morning light.
With roots in fun and branches in play,
A verdant friend who saves the day!

Whispers from the Fern

In the corner, ferns collide,
Whispers of green, a leafy ride.
A spider walks with a dodgy grin,
Plotting mischief where thoughts begin.

Feathers of green, they prance and sway,
Stretched arms beckon, come out to play.
Tiny voices sing, just a tease,
In the shade where sunlight flees.

One vine dreams of silk and lace,
While another curls, hiding its face.
They giggle and sway, a leafy row,
Plant pals share secrets they'll never know.

The wind whispers soft, a giggly spell,
Tales of the garden, antics to tell.
A bloom splashes color, a bold act,
In this green party, not one fact lacks!

A Dance of Chlorophyll

Under the sun, the plants will prance,
Conducting their symphony, a lively dance.
Leaves shimmy and sway, all in a row,
Two pots tango, putting on a show.

A cactus claps, but pricks a toe,
Hoping for friends to join in the flow.
"Let's root for each other," the daisies shout,
As a marigold fluffs, full of clout.

Photosynthesizing in vibrant hues,
All around, nature's joyful cues.
The twist and turn, their rhythm divine,
Wild and wacky but perfectly fine.

Laughter erupts from petals and leaves,
As the sun dips low, the chlorophyll weaves.
So dance little greens under the light,
In this party of plants, all feels just right!

Sprouts of Serenity

Tiny sprouts poke through the earth,
Laughing loudly, claiming their worth.
Each little plant has a quirky style,
Bringing joy with an innocent smile.

One sprout stretches, yawns, and sighs,
While another admires the cloudy skies.
Chasing sunlight, they twist and twirl,
In a mini-world where giggles unfurl.

With morning dew on parties supreme,
They gather around, sharing a dream.
Roots intertwine, a comical knot,
Who's tangled who? They've all forgot.

"Life is a garden," they chuckle and cheer,
Finding peace in laughter, year after year.
In shades of green, they settle down,
With humble hearts, they'll wear the crown.

Ciphers in the Soil

Buried secrets in dampened ground,
Whispers of wonders, not yet found.
Roots tap dance in their darkened abode,
Practicing tales, ages old.

Folks may ponder what lies beneath,
As optimistic sprouts giggle with ease.
In shadows, they plot, a riddle's embrace,
Life's vibrant chorus, a plant's embrace.

"Can we unearth treasures?" they tease and giggle,
Searching for goodies, with a little wiggle.
All the clues lead to fun in the dirt,
Where secrets bloom, and friendships assert.

An earthworm listens, quite bemused,
At the musings of greens, thoroughly fused.
While snails express, in their slow, sweet toil,
The joy of kinship—those ciphers in soil!

Hideaways of Harmony

In a corner, shyly tucked away,
A leafy friend has come to play.
With arms outstretched, they sway with glee,
Sipping sunshine, oh so free.

When guests arrive, it's time to hide,
Among the fronds, they safely bide.
With laughter loud, they shake and dance,
A leafy party, given a chance!

Each little leaf has tales to share,
Of sunlit days and friendly air.
They giggle softly, never shy,
As dust bunnies from couches fly.

So let them lounge, enjoy the fun,
In their leafy world under the sun.
For when you peek, you might just find,
A secret life, quite unconfined.

The Veins of Verdancy

Amidst the greens, a party brews,
With leafy friends and tiny shoes.
A dance of roots beneath the soil,
They twist and turn, without a toil.

Their veins, like roads, spread far and wide,
A highway for bugs to glide.
A parade of ants, a wormy feast,
In this verdant land, fun never ceased.

They tell the tales of rain and sun,
Through whispers shared, they laugh and run.
With every drop of morning dew,
Their joy spills over, bursting through.

As shadows stretch and daylight fades,
They settle down in leafy glades.
With a sigh and sleepy yawn,
Tomorrow's fun will soon be drawn.

Sanctuary of Petals

Nestled close, where petals bloom,
A secret spot dispels the gloom.
Here flowers gossip, chuckle too,
In colors bright, they steal the view.

With every swirl of fragrant air,
They throw confetti, without a care.
Bees and ants join in the cheer,
Wobbling wildly, but full of cheer.

Through sunny days, they share a laugh,
With cheeky chimes from the giraffe.
In every shade and fragrant hue,
This blossom tribe knows just what to do.

At dusk they twirl to evening's song,
In this sanctuary, they belong.
With twilight's grace, their giggles sway,
In perfect harmony, they play.

Breathing in the Green

In huddled heaps, they gather tight,
Little green sprites, oh what a sight!
They breathe in deeply, giggling loud,
In their green haven, always proud.

With ferny fronds that tickle toes,
And leafy hats with floppy bows.
Every inch, a joyful space,
Where laughter blooms in every place.

Flitting about, like bees on a spree,
They share their tales with pure glee.
In shoots and sprouts, their humor thrives,
Planting joy, where life derives.

So come, indulge, and take a seat,
In this green realm, oh what a treat!
For when you breathe in all that's seen,
You'll find the fun in all the green.

Greenhouse Chronicles

In the greenhouse, plants conspire,
Leaves whisper tales, never tire.
Potting soil and water dance,
The sun winks, giving plants a chance.

Froggy friends hop by with cheer,
Gossiping blooms, who knows what they're near?
With jokes and laughs, they stretch and sway,
Plant friends gather, sharing the day.

Dirt-covered hands, a badge of pride,
Each new leaf sprouts, they can't hide.
The air is thick with joyful vibes,
As seeds of laughter, the plant tribe scribes.

Compost heaps and birthday greens,
Fertilizer jokes, and garden scenes.
Each sprout a hoot, each pot a pun,
In this greenhouse, the fun's never done!

Arachne's Kin in the Corner

In the corner, a webbing queen,
Spinning jokes that are quite the scene.
Eight-legged laughter fills the room,
A tickle here, a giggle blooms.

Her plant pals sway, they join in the fun,
'The bigger the leaf, the better the pun!'
With each twist, a giggle grows,
In her silken threads, humor flows.

The potted plants chuckle and cheer,
Cracking up when the spider draws near.
Who knew they'd have a web of laughs,
As they curled up with their funny crafts?

A tangled web of jokes and cheer,
Each thread a laugh that we hold dear.
In this corner, giggles reign,
Arachne's kin, drop the mundane!

Nature's Hanging Symphony

Hanging high, the plants do sway,
A symphony of green on display.
Each leaf a note, each pot a drum,
In this green orchestra, the fun is yum!

Cacti chiming in with a poke,
The ferns flutter, sharing a joke.
As sunlight beams, the laughter grows,
Nature's concert, where humor flows.

The vines entwine like friends at play,
Whispering secrets to lighten the day.
Hanging low or climbing high,
In this lush world, none say goodbye.

With giggles rustling among the leaves,
Nature's harmony, everybody believes.
As roots dance beneath the cheerful hum,
In this hanging symphony, we all succumb!

Roots of Serenity

Beneath the soil, the roots take hold,
Sharing giggles, both brave and bold.
They tickle the ground with a soft embrace,
In the underworld, they find their place.

The fungi cheer, 'We're in this together!'
The roots weave stories, light as a feather.
They lift the plants with every grin,
Making the garden a peaceful din.

Laughing worms wiggle with delight,
Telling secrets in the warmth of night.
From deep below, to the sun above,
In this world, we share the love.

With roots grounded, laughter takes flight,
A serene scene, pure and bright.
In the soil, a joyful spree,
A community where we're all carefree!

Nature's Hidden Treasures

In corners of homes, they often reside,
With leaves like green spears, they try to hide.
Water them gently, they giggle with glee,
Little green wonders, a jungle for free.

They dangle like starlings, a whimsical sight,
In a battle of growth, they bring pure delight.
Chasing the sunlight, they sway to and fro,
Nature's own jugglers, putting on a show.

Their babies come falling, a family affair,
Hitching a ride on the wind like a dare.
Collect them in pots, let your gardens expand,
Who knew little plants had such a big band?

So raise up your glasses, to greenery's charm,
These leafy companions mean no one harm.
With laughter and sunshine, they flourish and play,
Nature's best jesters brighten the day.

Life Entwined

In every small room, joy curiously spreads,
With vines as their ropes, they weave leafy threads.
They dance on the windowsills, chasing the sun,
A happy parade, oh what fun to be spun!

Each leaf tells a story, of mischief and glee,
Of pots full of dirt and wild dreams to be.
Hiding from dust bunnies, making them flee,
Our leafy companions, as funny as can be!

They grow with a flair, a comedic intent,
Twisting, turning, they don't pay rent.
They giggle in silence, who knew plants could tease?
In the game of life, they do it with ease.

So let's plant some laughter, and nourish with care,
For life's little treasures are often laid bare.
With love on our side, and greenery's might,
We intertwine lives, making everything bright.

Echoes of Earth

Whispers of green in the gentle breeze,
Plant babies frolicking, doing as they please.
From a single small leaf, a forest can grow,
Echoes of laughter in the sunlight's glow.

They stretch and they reach for the sky's embrace,
In a leafy ballet, they dance with such grace.
A comedy show with nature's own cast,
With each goofy leaf, our hearts are amassed.

In pots full of charm, they wiggle and sway,
Each twist and turn makes the onlookers stay.
Little green jesters, by windows they wink,
A symphony of green, let's pause and think.

So raise up your hands to the roots underground,
For life's hidden treasures in laughter are found.
With giggles in harmony, by nature's decree,
The echoes of earth are as funny as can be!

Garden Guardians

In patches of green, they proudly defend,
Guardians of laughter, around every bend.
With leafy armor, they stand tall and bright,
Ready to giggle through day and through night.

Their roots dig deep, in a soil so sweet,
Tickling each toe, with every small feat.
They rally for sunshine, like soldiers of cheer,
In the glorious garden, where plants persevere.

As pets without fur, they bring joy our way,
With characters quirky, they steal hearts each day.
They nod at the flowers, exchanging their jokes,
In a world of green laughter, joy simply evokes.

So plant your own heroes, let the fun begin,
In the theater of growth where the giggles spin.
With each little shoot, your heart will expand,
These garden guardians are simply grand!

Secrets of the Climbing Vine

A leafy labyrinth climbs so high,
It plots its course to the sky.
With tiny pot and roots galore,
It whispers tales of what's in store.

A squirrel once thought it was a tree,
And took a nap, just for a spree.
But vines are sly, and soon he'd find,
He's trapped in leaves, oh how unkind!

The cat conspirators sit and stare,
What game is this? They stop and share.
In silent giggles, they conspire,
Who'll be the first to climb up higher?

With every twist, it twirls and bends,
Creating paths, as if it trends.
The secrets of nature take the floor,
In a pot of fun, who could want more?

Serenity in Each Leaf

In rooms where peace prefers to play,
A gentle whisper from green ballet.
Leaves like laughter flutter and sway,
Serenity found in a plant's display.

It sits on shelves, proud and bold,
Guarding secrets that it has told.
Each leaf a story, a funny plot,
A comedy act in a sunny spot.

When dust gathers, it gives a wink,
Saying, "Hey, I need a drink!"
A spritz of water, and there it beams,
With joy that bursts like happy dreams.

Invite your friends to gather 'round,
To share in laughter where joy is found.
This simple green, with tales so sweet,
Makes every day feel like a treat!

Nature's Embrace within Four Walls

Inside these walls, green fingers creep,
While we giggle, it too loves to leap.
It lulls us gently with its grace,
Each leaf a smile, a cozy place.

When guests arrive for tea and cheer,
Vines hilariously draw them near.
Startled, as if to say, "Surprise!"
They laugh out loud at nature's guise.

A party plant, it spins with glee,
Making our home a leafy spree.
With every sip, it seems to sway,
As if to say, "Let's dance today!"

So here we are, in laughter's hold,
With nature's whimsy, bold and gold.
Within these walls, let joy entwine,
For every leaf has its own shine.

Dance of the Indoor Wanderer

The wanderer roams from pot to pot,
A curious soul, so spry and hot.
With each little move, it seems to dance,
Spreading joy like a pure romance.

From corner to corner, it twists and twirls,
A leafy ballet that makes us swirl.
"Hey there!" it nods with a cheeky grin,
Who knew houseplants could make you spin?

The cat joins in with a pounce and leap,
Together they swirl, a fun little heap.
A dance party here, in our cozy nook,
Where plants are the stars of the funny book.

So let's all giggle and turn with flair,
As leaves and paws float through the air.
An indoor party, just us two,
Where fun is grown and laughter too!

www.ingramcontent.com/pod-product-compliance
Lightning Source LLC
Chambersburg PA
CBHW070318120526
44590CB00017B/2724